I0098038

# GODDESS UNDER THE BRIDGE

## POEMS
### DuEwa Frazier

# GODDESS
# UNDER
# THE BRIDGE

POEMS

Lit Noire Publishing

New York

*books by duewa frazier*

deanne in the middle (forthcoming 2013)

ten marbles and a bag to put them in:
poems for children (2010)

check the rhyme:
an anthology of female poets & emcees (2006)

stardust tracks on a road (2005)

shedding light from my journeys (2002)

**Published by**
Lit Noire Publishing
P.O. Box 26183
Brooklyn, NY 11201

Copyright © 2006-2013 DuEwa Frazier
Manufactured in the United States of America

Editor: Angela Jackson-Brown

1st Edition Paperback

No part of this publication may be reproduced, stored in a retrieval system, or transmitted in any form or by any means, electronic, mechanical, photocopying, recording, scanning, or otherwise accept by written permission of the publisher.

Library of Congress Control Number: 2013934038

Goddess Under the Bridge / DuEwa Frazier
ISBN-10: 0971905282
ISBN-13: 978-0-9719052-8-3
　　　I.　　　Frazier, DuEwa

Printed in the United States of America

10 9 8 7 6 5 4 3 2 1

*For lost and found goddesses and
wild women everywhere.*

# Acknowledgements

"Afterthoughts" was previously published in Poetry in
Performance #37 (CUNY-The Poetry Center)

"Guarantee" was previously published in
Poetry Ink Anthology (Plan B Press)

"What Light Looks Like" was previously published in
Kweli Journal

"Blues River" was previously published in Tidal Basin Review

## *Thank you*

I wish to thank my loved ones for their support. I wish to thank my artistic mentors and my colleagues in the fields of writing, education, performance art and publishing. I thank the artist Jewell Golden who once told me, "When we create, we have an angel artist who sits down and creates alongside us." Golden's inspiring statement helped me remember that magic and divinity is never far from our midst when creativity is at work.

I also thank: The New School MFA in Creative Writing program, Cave Canem Regional Workshops, Poets & Writers, Inc., Hue Man Bookstore, The Harlem Book Fair, Pattie Carragon and Brownstone Poets, Queens Library, Morningside Alliance Read Out Loud, The Links, Inc. – Queens Chapter, Hampton University Alumni and my editor, Angela Jackson-Brown.

DuEwa Frazier
New York
2013

*Salute to:*

**Augustwilson**majorjacksonthomassayersellissuzanloripark-serykahbadujohncoltrane**lucilleclifton**hakimadhubutialice-walkersapphirentozakeshange**soniasanchez**shaktigawainmi-chaeljacksonmarvingayegeorgeclintonalgreentherootseric-bandrakimmclyteursularuckerladybugmeccajillscotturtsu-laruckerthelastpoetstonymedina**pearlcleage**truththoma-sandmanymore...thankyouforinspiringmethroughyourart.

# Contents

# GODDESS
# POEMS

## Gypsy (for Lucille Clifton)

My spirit collected memories
From Mississippi
A journey
I could never forget
Ancestors threatened to call me home
I rode on the back of my great grandmother:
A Native American, an African, a woman with metal
In her core
I could never stop moving, once a gypsy
Always a gypsy
Trained to survive from the center of my mother's garden
I was a child of a mother, not a father
A delayed genius, a fearful porcupine
I change my colors depending on
Who I have to fight next

◆ ◆ ◆

## *Unequally Yoked*

You followed my scent
an enticing danger
you weren't strong enough
to handle
when you entered you didn't
recognize that
my cave has guardians
always watching and protecting

You have always known me
I was the yellow feather
floating over your head
the dog barking in the night
the burning in your stomach
the old woman's sound advice
an enticing danger
you never wanted to kiss with your eyes closed
afraid of my conjure
your lack of depth became my boredom

I tried in vain to introduce
you to my tribe
you were never in danger of becoming
who I needed, your constitution wasn't
built for that
you weren't in love with ritual or righteousness
I wasn't in love with ambiguity or secrecy

We were unequally yoked

A part of my soul you kept
I'll get it back
when I see you
next lifetime

♦ ♦ ♦

# Pay the Goddess for Love

right before the moon eclipsed the sun
& before 9 months of rain
we tried, in vain
to pay the goddess for love

harmony eluded us
me, your good girl
you, my dark cloud
the one I could never escape

*pour the honey in the mississippi*

emotional unraveling
eventual rejection
too much pride swallowed us
you never understood the goddess

it takes patience and humility
to partner with feminine genius
our miracle was never meant to happen

◆ ◆ ◆

## *riding the market street L*

Late for work
a million thoughts piled on top
of a million other thoughts

I am raccoon girl
dark shiny circles around my eyes
no sleep until Brooklyn

I try to hear myself
my Ori is an antennae picking up way too many
frequencies, voices and emotions

I create noise
no one hears
I am on edge
On the brink of - losing it

I am screaming inside
a lost child
pleading for someone to find me

◆ ◆ ◆

## Don't Leave Me

don't leave me –
tied up in myself
clutching your pillow
crying myself to sleep
muttering, cluttered mind
waiting for you at the door
chained to your neglectful ways
sucking the rancid remnants of your love
breast and flower swelled
with half of my spirit still with you
money gone, house gone & food gone
giving what little I have away
with sunken eyes & closed mouth
in what I wore yesterday & the day before
womb screaming and terrified
full with child
whispering your name like a prayer
before I grow wings & sprout courage to say
goodbye

◆ ◆ ◆

# Guarantee

Life has no guarantees
you told me
but today I am in need
of a down payment
for guarantee, that is

Summer comes
you are ripe in this season
like a crisp pear
or juicy mango

You are not exotic
I have seen your kind before
cool to the core
exciting to touch
mesmerizing to watch
I want to grasp the meaning of you
but it is hard to study a book
that never talks
I need the metaphors, the imagery
and words that signify
to play this game

I will not be your
good luck charm
I have given too much away
with no guarantee – ever
in sight

◆ ◆ ◆

## Woman what have you done? (for 5-year old Shaniya)

She must have been on drugs,
to sell her child I thought.
The man, caught on tape carrying the
little girl in his arms in the hotel.
What the hell was he doing with her?
Why did her mother sell her and send her with this man?
What is the world coming to?

*Somebody's calling my name*
*Oh Mary*
*Somebody's calling my name*
*St. Peter*
*Somebody's calling my name.*
*Sweet Jesus*
*Somebody's calling my name.*
*Yemaya*
Woman this child was from your womb
Wy did you leave her?

This child was in your care.
Wy did you sell her?
This child was not yours to abuse.
Why did you give her over to evil?

What kind of spirits surround you?
Wy did you not consider the consequences?
This baby was in the custody of her father.
Why didn't you let her stay there?
Why did you have to be a black sista?
Why did you have to be a low down sista?
Our hearts weep for you.
Our hearts weep for the baby.
We want you to make it right.
We want you to be forgiven
We want you to not do this to your unborn child.
We know addiction causes poor judgment.
Did you have to sell your five-year old baby?
Her daddy will not see her grown up.

Her auntie will not see her grown up.
She will never have best friends.
She will never go to college.
She will never travel the world.
Woman she will never get married.
She will never kiss her children to sleep.
She will never be an elder.
She is gone, gone, gone now.

◆ ◆ ◆

## dirt, the imposter

the snake in my mouth commands you

to stop stealing

manipulating

& searching

me out

you are not my sista, conniving dirt bitch

want what I got but don't know my code

I digitize     my divine blueprint     in technology

too righteous for you     to read

I dust     daughter

& sekhmet goddess complex

you perplexed walking around stalking me

riding me     you studying me

to find how I get what I got

I was born under the sun

on the 1st day

I am lioness, tiger woman huntress

I naturally manifest

I play no games     I am original     one who cannot be played

I am liberated woman, not a slave

you are not trained   for combat with   me

I naturally multiply   my destiny     by the power of 3

you are not my sista, conniving dirt bitch

move on to your underground playground

stay on your side of town

before I

blow you

away

◆ ◆ ◆

# pine

100 degrees
*must not fall*
*make it to the building in one piece*
I can't calm it - my heart
Leo rules the heart, the spine and circulation
a spiritual problem, manifesting as a physical one
drowning in fear
my heart races over a hundred beats per minute
there is not enough oxygen
I am floating
I look up
I don't recognize my own sky
the pressure in my head is enormous
my Ori is tapping me
I am not in control
I am so tired
I can't go home, I'd be a failure
I am a tightly woven ball of thread
hoping to get out of the hell I created

◆ ◆ ◆

## angel on Lancaster

*lean on me*
*when you're not strong*
love comes in many forms
people who know what love
is give it freely
I knew you were a wise woman
when I met you
public libraries often host
lost souls and angels
people whose only possible
friends are books
I was the lost soul
you , the angel
you treated me as if I were your
daughter, when your own daughter
was away
you told me I had power, but I didn't  know it

orange was the dominant color in your place
your living room reached out to hug me
when I entered
it was a safe place, filled with your art
and filled with love
you taught me to own my power

you helped me understand the
pain butterflies go through
because you are one
you knew I needed a friend, a listening
ear and a place to get quiet and still
you were not my blood, but you treated me
a million times better
I still have the journal you gave me for my birthday
when it was time for me to leave the city
you gave me your blessing
my sacred friend
you were an angel when I needed one
I will never forget the solitude you gave me

♦ ♦ ♦

## reading from the priestess

gain weight girl
if you don't
you won't be able to have children
you are very smart
get a phd
leave men alone
keep them as friends
the ancestors are yelling at you
BE HAPPY!
you are so afraid
you need to open up
if you don't
you will be alone
your mother, pray for her
continue to pray for your
whole family

all the nervous energy you feel
you need to channel it into metal
think of ogun
you are strong
build yourself up
this thing, this culture, this religion
did not make you feel good about
yourself
you need to find out what does
{{{Poetry!!!!!!!}}}

◆ ◆ ◆

## *troll witch*

underneath your clothes
you are not a woman
a teacher
a healer
a peacemaker
a leader or
a diva

every word from
your mouth
is broken glass that cuts
a fungus surrounds you, arrows point
at you and your misfortune
feces spills out of your ears

no enlightenment lives inside you
lacking education (real or imagined)
and tact
and couth
and sweetness
and diplomacy
you are the opposite of poetic

you serve on behalf of no one
your position was given out of
familial obligation
your foundation is a rotten root
too weak to hold you up

my eloquence and motivation
was too much for your black heart
you surrounded by demons
I surrounded by light
I dwell in possibilities and inspired visions
You dwell in lack and limited ability
You are banished
my prayers bind your poison

beware of my guardians
they will bite you

◆ ◆ ◆

# *A Queen Has Arrived (for Michelle Obama)*

Our dreams for you are the ones
we have for ourselves
We understand your no nonsense flair
your serious credentials
and the slick way your wear your hair


We admire you for not wanting to be like every other first lady
who was like every other first lady who was like every other first
lady
We are proud of the man Barack, but we
revere the woman, Michelle
Goddess
-woman/daughter/mother/wife/intellectual/friend/attorney/
executive/and every woman's girl friend
A Queen has arrived
How we smiled and cried when the election was won
How we cried and smiled when you moved into that big house


No more jokes about what black folks would do if they were in
the White House – we know all about it – because you're there
and we are proud
How we smiled when we saw you breaking ground, planting an
organic garden with the children, getting our kids to move
How we said go 'head girl with your bad self when you bared
your shoulders and arms at the Inaugural Ball and then again at

The State Dinner

How we've defended you when news media and conservatives have lost their mind, attacking our first African American first lady

How we've held our breath, praying that no harm be done to you or your family during this exciting yet stressful time

"Michelle My Belle" is the name of the song

Girl from the Southside of Chi-town, you came along way, a long way to where you belong

Destiny opened up for you and yours


Malia and Sasha have a Queen to look up to, they should be proud

Michelle we speak you

well

happy

proud

standing tall

graceful

peaceful

smart

humble

powerful

striking

nurturing

inspiring

Michelle when you shine, we all shine

We thank you for reflecting the beauty, strength, power, grace
and intelligence that we knew we had all along

Go 'head with your beautiful self!

◆ ◆ ◆

# Jazz Mystic (for Alice Coltrane)

### 1.

*Journey In Satchidananda*
Raise hair on my neck
Harp let out ancestor cry
Wrap around humanity
Chords make flowers bloom
Beneath frozen ground
Run through the earth
Make a pathway to heaven

### 2.

You & your mate, King John
Played & lounged in
My parents' living room in Queens
I was five

Not knowing your love would
Become a part of me
Your music, a familiar chant
Entered our home often

Neither sadness nor strife
Could dwell there
When you came
To visit

3.
The 22nd day of October, 2006
NJPAC concert
in Newark, New Jersey
On a warm, fall evening

I walk through the reception
Soak up the spirit
Of oneness in the room
Smile at Cornel West & other notables

All are here to rest
At your feet for awhile
Celebrate you
A legend named Coltrane

I sit, on the edge of my seat
Like an anxious child
My heart leaps from the balcony
To greet you
There you are, Swamini
Adorned in orange sari, flecked with gold
You glide onto the stage
Conjure the divine

Ravi on sax, DeJohnette on drums
Gress & Workman on bass
Unifying the magnificent
Sounds of your organ and piano

Led by your ashram choir
Meditation welcomed us into
Sacred reflection
As we journey into *Translinear Light*

Immersed in your universe
We forget ourselves
We are the lucky ones
Anointed by your gift

◆ ◆ ◆

## *What Light Looks Like (for Pearl Cleage)*

Looks like a sister
in solitude
serenading herself
love on the horizon

Looks like jazz piano
at dawn
steam coming off a pot of
simmering collard greens
on Sunday morning
Looks like a woman
fed up
who will only accept
the best part of good
& genuine warmth from
her lover
Looks like meditation at
the ocean
the body relaxing in its glistening skin
leaving madness behind
& eating mangos and coconut in warm places

Looks like a champion for children
an artist catching truth
before it turns the corner into a lie

Looks like celebration of
the present
visualizing heart chakra healing
exploding into pink and red wild roses
Looks like cherishing
women's work
honoring an elder
dancing with the Spirit
shaking hands with moon magic
& sacred embrace never ending

◆ ◆ ◆

## Cowgirls (for Suzan Lori Parks)

We remixed Wilson, Hansberry, Baldwin and Hurston
To create you
You stomped on our fright
Loosed our woulda coulda shoulda excuse
Rock and rolled us with your third eye vision
The way only a bad sister can
So we became your clan

There are few of us left
Wild women waking to use art as ritual
Hips rumbling when we walk
Bellies and wombs full of our prose
Hair connecting with roots of ancestor scribes
Carrying wisdom of the Tao in our hands

We are wiser than generations before
We know amethyst, lapis lazuli, carnelian and onyx
Are more precious than diamonds

We writerhymetotelltimeandtellitlikeitis
Yo! Word! BLING!
We are beyond mediocrity
We are beyond complacency
We earth, wind, fire, water goddesses
Healing broken ones to the Nth degree

We burn buildings with our brightness
We next generation warriors jacking sky
We fly

We settle this new frontier birthing new daughters
Who got next on the stage
We locked, loaded and lettered
We healers at the podium recording language
Then playing it back
Rotating images you can read, notes you can sing

We transform ourselves into digital rainbows
Fighting the power
Bringing that beat back

◆ ◆ ◆

# Club Viva (St. Louis, 1998)

Thursday night is ladies night
Shake, salsa, soca, self seduction
your troubles away

Mami wear gold, yellow, orange or red
let your feet make fire
have your hands held
your hips turned
your body twirled
your shoulders shimmied

Let the music fill your soul
& transport you to other places
like
**A**rgentina
**B**razil
**C**uba

Jam like you are part of the band
reflect the Goddess
Oshun is your guide
Loving life on the dance floor

◆ ◆ ◆

## *Teacher With a Bad Attitude (Class)*

Students walk in the classroom & say, *I ain't doing no reading,
writing, discussing or learning today*

Teacher asks, *Why?*

Students say, *Cause I don't feel like it*

Teacher says, *Open your books you don't have time to play*

Students say, *I'm tired/hungry/hurt/itching/bored/pissed
off/& angry*

Teacher says, *Well go see the counselor/social worker/nurse/ap/
principal/or monitor in the hallway (or well why did you even
come to school today?)*

Students say, *Cause my mama/grandmama/daddy/uncle/cousins/
sister/brother made me (teacher writes all of this down in an
anecdotal notebook)*

Students say, *That witch stole my cell phone/play station/
metrocard/ipod/basketball/noisemaker/balloon/chris brown-lil
wayne-trey songz cd/lipgloss/$50 bill/photo album/ &boyfriend*

Teacher says, *If it happened on school grounds, write a letter to the principal/security guard/monitor in the hallway or settle it in a mature way yourself (teacher doubts they can settle anything in a mature way)*

Students say (to the teacher), *You ain't gon' take my cell phone/playstation/purse/metrocard/ipod/basketball/noisemaker/ ballon/chris brown-usher-beyonce cd/lip gloss/$50 bill/photo album/boyfriend*

Teacher says, *Yes I will take it if you don't put it away and focus on your work*

Students say, *I hate all teachers, all y'all teachers is corny & say the same things,none 'o' y'all know nothing, can't wait to get out of this school*

(no they don't mean leaving by graduating from the school)

Teacher says, *I have my education, now you have to get yours, if you continue to be disrespectful I'm going to write you up*

Student says, *Write me up, I don't wanna be in this school no way...I'm leavin'*

Teacher thinks, *Good*

◆ ◆ ◆

# Writing the Change Poem

"The theme for this poem is change"
I tell my students
"I'd like you to reflect upon who you were
last year and who you would like to be this year.
Ask yourself: What can I improve0 upon in myself and my life?
What do I want to do differently? This is my change poem,
you can use it as your model"

Marlon replied, "Writing poetry is too personal.  I can't do it!"
Nadia had so much to write she said her poem
"Can't be limited to just one page Ms. Frazier"
Darnell's change poem revealed
that he was not interested in school last year
but he knows he wants to "do better this year"

Arlon stares into space
tapping his pen against his desk's surface
"Arlon are you okay? Do you need help?" I ask him
"No, I'm just thinking," he replied.
Freddie said he "used to be out of control"
But now he's "ready to be calm and focused"
Danielle wants to be more positive about her life
despite the fact that she is 14 and has painful bouts of
arthritis

Mavis admitted that she is "too shy"
Vaughn realized he has a temper and
needs to do something about it
Sharon said that she is "too loud" and will
try to speak more softly
These are my students
they have learned how to self reflect
as they look forward they see that
change is inevitable

♦ ♦ ♦

# Goddess Under the Bridge

fix your hair girl

sho is wild and just blowin in this here wind

wipe the drip running down your legs

put some of them stars back on your shoulders

you got too many flies buzzing around your head

fix your skirt, it's got holes in it

and your socks is dirty

where you been walking at chile?

teeth is yellow and cracking too, lawd

you ain't got nuff teeth to eat wit

nor press no man wit

you gotta mouth and that's what I want

you to lead wit

but you don't use it

give me the coins and the dollar

pay me all of it

all you got

gather shells and sea water
I need some fruits too
I want me some oranges and some
mango and some of them tangelos
bring me some honey
whole big ole
jar of honey
carry it in your mouth
your bittersweet closed mouth
And I want a horse
a horse so I can run away
get out of here when the fire
comes
I want me a horse, no I want
seven horses
seven horses, one for each
day and I'm gone name 'em
after each of my seven children
they all gone

and you all I got now
my good luck charm
my rubbing rock
my rain stick
my dream catcher
and since you wanna know so bad
you won't never know
what I gone give you back
you won't never know
just might be a sword, a tree, a river
or a mountain
if you earn it

◆ ◆ ◆

## *No More Muse-ik*

I will not sell myself to you
for love, nor beg you to stay
Your non committal wage cannot afford my
heart's hourly rate

I do not miss your sometime
offering of boyish, forgetful love
You didn't know how to be a man
I'm no mama to raise you

I will not welcome you back
into my dreams
or give you my sensual sand
My fantasies consist of only me

I will not celebrate my born
day with you by my side
I will not smile and be peace

with your jump offs nearby
afros and braids glistening
wearing fake smiles

I am no longer your lyrical feline
dancing for you
dropping knowledge on you
You are no longer my muse
When I hear your music
I turn away - eyes too dry to cry

I have no milk for sons who are  not my babies
The hip hop you birthed in me no longer hoorays
My poetry will live on without you in my head

◆ ◆ ◆

## she spectacle

she spectacle talks too much
everyone knows what she thinks, who she knows
is addicted to
men, now & laters, lotto and poems
competes
even if it means killing herself
wears big hair, bright clothes
purple heels, dazzling mouth and hot pink toes
is mother to everyone's child
except her own
is whiny, hungry cats
in a forgotten home
was the youngest
still trying to get her mama's attention
imagine her dancing for a nickel
selling words, to keep from becoming dried bones

◆ ◆ ◆

## good hair

I want to be more beautiful
I want it to be manageable
I pay $70 to be more beautiful
for it to be more manageable

he puts the white chemical cream
on my hair
says it might burn
I feel nothing
I wait for beauty

warm water washes it all away
fingers rub, caress the scalp
warm water washes away
the cream
my hair
the beauty

my stylist's silly grin
my self esteem
tied to my good hair
crowning glory no more

he takes out the scissors
to make the damage appear
less visible

he blames it – the hair loss
on me
says I didn't come often enough

I say this is enough

I blame it – the hair loss
on him
he's the one who went to school
to do good hair

◆ ◆ ◆

# begin again

no mama to hold you in her arm
no hot boys tempting you to be bad
no blankets to keep you warm
no memories to make you sad

no guardian to watch your back
no priest to read your path
no consciousness to keep you black
no joke to make you laugh

no friends to welcome you
no car, train or bus to take you home
no mentor to believe in you
no song lyric or poem

no interpreter for language to learn
no attitude to check at the door
no position to earn

no child returning as ancestor
no ocean to bathe in salt water
no love-making to make you sing
no crystal to heal your aura
no trees to transform you green

no notification to make you wait
no music to make you dance
no psalms to build your faith
no suitor to share romance

no therapy to put your mind at ease
no poetry to write
no books to read
no enemies to fight

no words to rant
no goals to achieve
no affirmations to chant
no prayers to believe

time to begin again

◆ ◆ ◆

## *strange that you came*

i was hoping you
would be my
night in shining armor
i was told a long
time ago there aren't any left
you were more of
a princess than i ever was
looking for someone
to save you

strange that you came
after the night the yellow
candle burned
wanting love yet
not wanting any
"distractions" to your
own wants & outside pursuits
love needs its own space

and time
love cannot compete with
any others
you treated love like an irritation
a bothersome rash
a red stain on a crisp white shirt
or a harassing bill collector

i never fell in love with you
falling means stupidity
blindness
desperation
something an organized
person never falls for
you put me in touch
with a simple side
of myself
one that does not take

much thought, planning

or passion
but i need passion
life is not worth living
without it

you were a happening
i never really wanted
you were a boy
when i wanted a man

you didn't want to be a knight
in shining armor
i kept you
every silly, simple part of you
anyway

◆ ◆ ◆

## what women should do

women should
go to work mon thru fri
do laundry on sat
maybe rest on sun

women should
get married & have a baby
by 30

women should want
a man who brings home
his pay
women should smile,
be happy & stylish
in every way
women should never
talk or laugh too loud
and behave foolishly

women should not race
cars, play basketball, or
hang out in bars – you know
having fun a man's way

women can't ever get along
they're just too catty

or is that just what
"they" say?

♦ ♦ ♦

# *No Plants*

Stepping into the
sacred space of my love
for the first time

Key turns gently
into the lock
dark inside
a contrast to the light outside

We enter, stumble
thick brown rug
in the doorway has crept under the door

I am silent
waiting to be guided toward
my next step
using all my senses
I want to smell that clean & sweet
smell that lingers on his clothes

I reach for the light switch
can't feel it, I am impatient
He steps in front of me, turns the corner
from the hallway
light

I can see eight of the thirteen walls
that make up this
tiny little space

Thirteen walls
one kitchenette
one bedroom
one bath
two windows

No space to dance &
NO PLANTS! WHERE ARE THE PLANTS?!

thoughts scream & question
No plants
no fresh air
nothing to water
no time to care for anything besides himself
he does not want them for gifts
his mother never gave him one

neither did his neighbor
or his ex
Boxes everywhere
& all things related to music
& technology
The colors are hues of gray and brown
not my happy colors

We sit on the sofa, puts his arms around me
I look at the clutter

feel the absence
of chlorophyll and think
*Can I dream here?*

◆ ◆ ◆

## *Buddha in Brooklyn*

bohemian baring beautiful brown bodies
bopping down bergen
dealing dreams on dekalb
sitting sidity on stuyvesant
faking the funk on flatbush
living large loving nappy heads on lafayette
libraries, laundry mats, ladies named laylah
holding heavy heartbreak on halsey
african street festival in summer
saving souls sanctified at brooklyn tabernacle, st. paul,
emmanuel, brown memorial, bridge street, concord baptist and
ccc
subway soul stepping  seriously smiling, signifying and
swearing
soaking sun like you was still in Jamaica, Trinidad, Barbados,
Guyana, Ghana and Grenada
curious cats calmly coming 'round corners on Clinton
children pop locking and playing on porches

public schools, poetry cafes and playgrounds
paul robeson theatre
wise women walking, wearing wrap dresses on washington
rip roaring reggae, classic jazz, afro carib and hip hop sounds
in crown heights and bed stuy

trees and babies grow in fort greene and prospect park

mack daddies making their mating calls to the ladies

moshood, night of the cookers, cakeman raven, brooklyn

bodega and frank's place on fulton

mamas calling out third floor windows to boys named Jahlil,

Jerome, and Jason

morning meditation makes marvelous myrtle look magnificent

like manhattan

The rhythm of brooklyn is calling all the little buddhas to come

home

♦ ♦ ♦

# Tanka

Forest Park in spring
Moments of contemplation
Peace within my heart
Hear my name called in the breeze
Freedom always waiting

◆ ◆ ◆

# My Reflection: A Love Poem

Your name is my daily chant
Your tenderness removes my battle scars
I am wounded, your divinity mends me
I want to paint you inside my visions
Decorate the walls of your inner shrine
I want to add my music to your sacred colors
Teach you my rhythms until you sing
I want to speak to you in the tongues of ancestors
Carry your warmth with pride
I want to be your priority and your back up plan
I want to go back in time to know you in stages
See you grow from a boy to a man
Love all of your laughter and innocence
Guard your every move, catch you when you fall
And then come back to the present
So I can reminisce over you like Pete & C.L.
When you are hurting, I want to heal you with
The power of seven warrior goddesses
Be your night nurse, always there when you call
Like Ms. Ross, I don't need no cure
You are my love for all seasons
I am the nectar you've been waiting for

♦ ♦ ♦

# Elegy for Lost Youth
## (for Derrion Albert of Chicago)

Caught and surrounded, on a cold fall day
Angels wept
Darkness took shape

A lamb among wolves
You were not one of them
Yet they share your same skin

Hate hijacked the Spirit of love
Beaten, kicked and stomped
Soldiers in combat with themselves
They cannot see their reflection

Heartless children who ignore
The invisible hand of ancestor guides
Silence will not protect them
A child is dead

Mothers no longer bonded to their babies
No fathers to teach them to be men
They rebel without a purpose

The system will surely lock them in
The hell they have grown used to
Keep them fixed on thug fantasies

That cannot be called life

♦ ♦ ♦

## *Anoint Yourself: An Affirmation Poem*

You are precious
anoint yourself with these words:
I am precious
I am beautiful
I am a sight to behold
I am love
I am loving
Love surrounds me
I am luscious and pleasing to myself
I am beautiful from head to toe
I anoint myself

You are precious
anoint yourself while bathing:
I love my hair
My hair is beautiful
I love my head
My head is beautiful

I love my eyes
My eyes are beautiful
I love my nose
My nose is beautiful
I love my lips

My lips are beautiful
I love my face
My face is beautiful
I love my ears
My ears are beautiful
I hug myself
I anoint myself with my sacred touch
My body is beautiful

You are precious
anoint yourself with every deed:
I feed myself good and wholesome food

I adorn myself with comfortable, beautiful things
The spirits of love, joy, beauty, abundance, peace
and balance
live within me and surround me

I am open to all that is good and wonderful in this
world
I attract goodness
I am good
I am beautiful and whole in every way

❖ ❖ ❖

## Chicken, Grits & Gravy Love
## (with a side of misunderstanding)

I loved you baby
I loved you not baby

You changed me baby
You changed me not baby

Thought I blew your mind
but the grease wasn't hot enough
Naw wasn't hot enough for ya

Thought I was doing something special
but the syrup wasn't sweet enough for ya

Thought I was your one and only
but you was never lost
or lonely without me

I loved you baby
I loved you not baby

You changed me baby
You changed me not baby

I ain't your sister or your mama
your maid or your Missus
but what I want to know is
Did you ever love me?
Cause I sho' waited for you to tell me
Til it got late
& somebody else came 'round calling me
Suga baby like how I like
Grinning      showing plenty of teeth
& smiling like sunshine
spilling gold

◆ ◆ ◆

# *Afterthoughts*

She thought she wanted to have ten kids.
She thought she wanted to have ten kids with him.
She thought wrong.
Yes Lord.
She thought of babies.
Her babies – to hold, mold and love.
Then the fighting, then the pushing started.

Where did the love go?

She wanted to be optimistic.
She wanted him to be optimistic.
She had a baby.
A son.
She named him after a King.
Martin was his name.

He said HE was the only King in the house.
A king.

She was tired of fighting everyday.
She was tired of fighting and working.
He wouldn't work and he wanted more babies.
Another one?

She had another baby, this time a girl.
She wanted her to have more fire than she had.
She named her Shaka.
A girl.

She worries about her heart all the time.
She worries about her heart cause there's no more joy.
She has to be strong for her two kids.
Not ten.

She wants to have another baby.
She thinks another baby will bring them closer.
He says he is bored, ready to leave, quit.
Leave now?

◆ ◆ ◆

# The Winner

tired of running a race that is not hers
her body fell hoping to play dead.
maybe she could have been saved.
maybe she should have given summertime some room,
and danced awhile with a simple boy.
maybe she should have pursued less.
maybe her identity  would be different
not painful and forced.
all who knew her said she was a winner
the best there was. little did they know, fear
and hunger finally ate her soul.

◆ ◆ ◆

## Blues River

No one ever swims in the river
where cobblestones disappear.
Where Osun waits for honey and cinnamon
holding her mirror up for you to catch
a glimpse of your reflection in the waves.
Pay Yeye for a love blessing.

No one ever swims in the river
that separates St. Louis from East St. Louis.
Don't be caught in East Boogie after dark.
You do, you betta come strapped.

No one ever swims in the water
traveling from Louisiana to Minnesota
like ancestors during the Great
Migration. Mississippi songs called blues

floating on the backs of traveling souls.
Creating a world from hope.

No one ever swims in the mighty Mississippi River
unless to get swept away in time and never return.

◆ ◆ ◆

## Forever Never

I met a bull

Poised like a matador

Intent to train

Or maybe tame

He was cigar and cognac

Conjuring

Took my breath - away

Dizzying

Reached for my femininity

Divided up my parts

Dangerous

Had a limp – emotional one

Chivalrous monster

Full of sparkling teeth

Threatened to eat my soul

I, observer to my own demise

Take care of me – never

No one likes predictable

◆ ◆ ◆

# The Loop

Delmar is not as I left it. There are
no more brown girls calling themselves
punk. With bright shadowed eyes, wearing
bangles hoping to be the next lead singer
in a funk band called "Flex."
No more Spanish girls named Trudy giving free clothes
from a vintage store on a slow day. No more girls named Irina,
my Russian twin who sings *Crush on You* and *All Cried Out* in
perfect R&B pitch. No more boys named Al or Gene or Calvin
carrying boom boxes and break dancing on
Westgate. No more boutique owners named
Kalimba who African dance and give wise
advice. No more *Rocky Horror Picture Show*,
*Beat Street, The Last Dragon or Brother From Another*
*Planet* showing at The Varsity. Stale popcorn never
tasted so good. No more elderly women from some far
away Eastern European country walking slowly up
Enright, hands clasps behind them, smiling and muttering
to themselves. No more Native American women with
long red hair named Patty. Carrying a Colt-45 can in
one hand. Cigarette in the other. Wearing daisy dukes and house
slippers. Arguing with a man she used to call lover.
No more Zorba the Greek for the best gyros in all of St. Louis.

I was the lone brown girl, searching for self amongst a
bed of multi-colored roses.  Lost in a Red Sea of cultures,
Talking to
strangers, learning new languages.  Writing poetry in my head.

Me and Chuck Berry, we call this place – home.

◆ ◆ ◆

# St. Louis (Or What I Left Behind)

Where are those boys named Smokie, David and Ron? Summer boys with creased jeans and the whitest Nikes or Reeboks. Fresh. They were workers in a factory or maybe street pharmacists with baby mamas named 'Vette, Trecie and 'Chelle. Dreams. For them boys who might become the next Bernard or Ozzie playing the field. Or rapping Country Grammar. Some took a chance on Hollywood or New York. Bama. We never used that word. Gangster or Conscious? You knew what side you were on. The Hang. CBC dances. The Galleria. Skating at Saints on Wednesday and Sunday. White Castle lot in the city after Saints. Alpha step show. Red Sea on Friday. Good girls. Catholic school girls only date boys at CBC, Ritter or Ladue. Don't bring any babies home. Watch the company you keep. Never skip school with a friend who doesn't have your back. The Northside. Lazy days in a house full of Snipes. Love in the pockets. Tearful letters. A Big Mac and fries to take the pain away. Secrets and a friend named Deion. Episcopal baptism at All Saints. Ritual without soul. Rebirth. Solar Yoga on Saturday. Orisas by number and color. The Odu. Psalms – 23, 27 and 91 for protection. Heartbreak. A man who would be a priest.

Leaving St. Louis.

Lit Noire Publishing

For more information:
www.duewaworld.com
Twitter.com/duewa1

www.ingramcontent.com/pod-product-compliance
Lightning Source LLC
Chambersburg PA
CBHW051848040426
42447CB00006B/758